Cost of the Cross

For information address

J2B Publishing LLC
4251 Columbia Park Road
Pomfret, MD 20657
www.J2BLLC.com
GladToDoIt@gmail.com

Cover and interior photographs by Benjamin Yates Brewster, Jr.

Printed and bound in the United States of America

ISBN: 978-1-948747-20-2

Cost of the Cross

Richard I. Gold

J2B PUBLISHING

Also by Richard I. Gold

God's Agenda: Religious Poems - Vol. I

Mary's Lamb and other Christmas Poems

God's Love - Easter Poems

Sayings for the Believer

Work is a 4-Letter Word

Free Advice

Life is a Trip

Dedication

My thanks to my wife who has helped me with the initial review and to those who have reviewed this work over time.

Table of Contents

COST OF THE CROSS

Everything in life has a cost
Whether great or small
We must pay the cost
When our creditors call

But there are debts we cannot pay
No matter how we try
Debts to other people
Debts to the One in the sky

The debts to the One above
Are debts for evil we do
When we cross the line
Are to His teachings untrue

But He paid the debt for us
A debt for which we're at a loss
The debt He paid for us
Was paid upon the cross

But what was the cost of this
It was God's only Son
Who came and lived and taught
God's only, Holy One

There was a payment in full
An advocate for us in need
To save us from the second death
Who for us He doth plead

The pain that Jesus did bear
For us may seem a loss
But you see, this was
The cost of the cross

THE CROSS OF CHRIST

There are many sins we do
We are but human kind
There is no holy excuse
When we are eternally judged

There is no forgiveness of sin
Except by the sheading of blood
Then our sins may be forgiven
By the Holy One above

The blood must be of something
Which we cherish and hold dear
If it is just killing something
That doth not relieve our fear

BUT GOD

But God sent His only Son
To die for you, for me
So that, before the Judge
It'll be heaven's gate we'll see

The death was not an easy one
The death upon a cross
For God loved us, and we must love Him
For saving us from eternal loss

So we must love our Lord
Our Lord upon the tree
Where our precious Lord
Died for you and me

THE LITTLE CROSS AT THE SIDE OF
THE ROAD

You pass it a hundred times
Thinking nothing of what it means
Just a fixture in the grass
A decoration among the green

But one day it hits you
The meaning of this cross
It was where cars did collide
Someone's life was lost

Was it a teenager
The hope for the future
Was it someone from a school
Perhaps a teacher

A moment's glance
A little to drink
A little nodding
All gone in a blink

We plan for the future
A future bright and fair
But for those signified by the cross
The future was not there

SALVATION IS THE GIFT OF GOD

Salvation is the gift of God
To those whom He doth give
Our quest for grace
Determines how we may live

We worship what we do not truly know
The face of God we cannot see
But by His power and by His grace
We will with Him forever be

So pray to God with all your heart
Love Him with mind and body and soul
For when we find grace in His sight
His power will make us whole

THE CHRISTIAN'S SALVATION

For the Christian who lives here
The world offers many a diversion
From the straight and narrow way
From the way of salvation

The temptations are many
Tugging on the strings of our heart
It would be so nice and easy
To let go and take part

But God's salvation is not easy
Few there are the way to find
The path that leads to heaven
There the devil to bind

SALVATION

The life of us upon this earth
Is but a fleeting time
There is no stopping our life's end
This is not an eternal crime

But God has, in His great love
Given us a holy way
So that when the end does come
We can rejoice on that glorious day

The Son of God came to us
To show us God's Holy Way
So that after the end of life
For our sins we will not have to pay

But the way of God
Starts not then, but now
For Jesus taught us the way
The living, the holy now

The path of life is the way
To walk as we live
Love as God doth love
As we are given, give

So gird up your strength
Give your very soul
To the holy One above
Who will make you whole

We are both body and mind
We must ourselves attain
The best of the holy way
It will not our selves strain

For the yoke of Christ is easy
A way to truly live
That in the end of it all
Eternal life to give

THERE IS BUT ONE WAY OF SALVATION

There is but one way of salvation
That way is set by God
It is all that matters
When you're beneath the sod

Salvation comes through faith
Faith in God's only Son
That at the end of this life
You will see God
After your life's race has run

But faith is one we must act
Must guide our every thought
This is not the easy way
That God's will has wrought

For actions make us
What we are
Bad actions
Will us from heaven bar

GOD BLESS YOU

God bless you
Is more than goodby
It is a hope
That God will be nigh

God bless you
And all that you have
For you need God's blessing
In order to survive

God bless you
In all that you do
And to God's will
May you ever be true

God bless you
May you know His grace
And when your life's complete
May your see his face

TO HEAR THE VOICE OF GOD

One day Moses was walking
Herding his father-in-law's sheep
When from a burning bush
He heard the Lord God speak

Moses was a man of wrath
Who had another killed
When he was walking out
He was not with religion filled

But God spoke to him
With a voice that he could hear
The message filled Moses with awe
With a mission and with fear

So God can speak to others
When they are not looking for Him
They must heed His voice
When He has a mission for them

If you should hear God's voice
Listen to what it has to say
For God is the prime power
Ignore it and you will have to pay

WHAT IS THE TIME TO WORSHIP GOD

What is the time to worship God
Morning, noon or night
We go to God in prayer
To seek His holy light

What is the time to pray
The past, the future or now
To seek God's holy guidance
To learn His holy how

Every time is the time to worship God
Every time is the time to pray
Carry His holy presence
Through both night and day

COME TO THE LIGHT

Come, come, come to the light
Leave the darkness behind
The light will dispel all evil
Will clear the clouded mind

Let no one stop you now
Let no one despair
For the joy of living
Will be with you there

No one can fully see
No one can understand
The message the light doth give
The love within His hand

Rewards for those who do right
Love, justice and the Lord
Follow His Holy example
Live by His Holy Word

SPIRIT OF THE LIVING GOD

Spirit of the living God
Father, Spirit and Son
To you is the victory
The many battles won

Come down to us, we pray
Teach us what to do
That to Your holy will
We may be forever true

There is Your path for us
The way that we must trod
It is the path of life
That leads to the feet of God

THE BEAUTY OF THE MOUNTAINS

The beauty of the mountains
Raising all around
Reminds us of God's glory
His blessings abound

We go to the mountains
The greatness to see
The ancient of days
Our place to be

To the top we go
What a view
Seeing God's nature
Makes all things new

CRY NOT

Cry not for those who are dead and gone
Have passed to the other side
In a new and different state
They have nothing to hide

They are beyond the reach of pain
Beyond life's worries and cares
They have begun their eternal journey
Upon heaven's golden stairs

Their bodies are no longer here
Buried beneath the sod
Their soul looks up
Upon the face of God

WE LIVE LIFE

We live life every day
We live as we would
But when the bill comes due
We wish we had lived as we should

We would know what is right
But we live as others guide
When it comes to respond
The way we traveled was easy and wide

So let us find the way
Let us follow the Holy One
That when we at last we see
The heavenly way was won

YOU'RE NOT A NOBODY

"You're not a nobody
You're a child of God"
So the church sign read
From now till we're beneath the sod

The Bible calls you a son
An heir to the throne
A leader without doubt
One who's good deeds should be known

Before you inherit the throne
You must face a cross
For what in this life is gain
May turn into eternal loss

If you have faith
You are your Heavenly Father's child
When you stand before His face
On you He'll give His holy smile

GIVEN THAT ALL WHO LIVE

Given that all who live
Are those who will eventually die
We must ask ourselves
Why is it we should try

No one likes to think of death
Of not being here
It is not the devil we know
As the unknown we fear

By faith we face the future
That when we cross the great divide
We will be in a better place
Over on the other side

NOW IT IS

The time has come
The die is cast
And men are sold for naught
The wrath of God goes forth
Within His grace
The souls of men He bought

The old is here
The future near
As time weaves it's eternal way
But men must know
As through life they go
It'll be the very devil we have pay

For time is where
Our soul draws near
To the eternal way
That we may learn
Our spirit churn
That which God doth say

WE LIVE ON A LINE

We live on a line of time
Beginning on the day of birth
It lasts as long as we live
Through sorrow and mirth

Ends on the day we die
To heaven we would go
The hope and assurance we have
Our eternal salvation we know

THE DIFFERENCE

We live our life within the world
Of some things we must partake
So that we may live from day to day
In this no difference we can make

But as we walk our walk in life
There is a road on which we must go
So that those about us will notice
That we are Christian, they will know

For if we are a Christian
We must different be
So that Christ may shine in us
His Holy Light others will see

THE WAY OF GOD

We live our lives as we would
Our life is our walk
We may know what we should do
But sometimes it's just talk

When meeting with others
It's easy to talk the talk
But in our heart of hearts
We need to walk the walk

The highest and the most noble
Is the Way of God
It will lead us all the way
To heaven when we're beneath the sod

I'M NOT YET READY

I'm not yet ready
To cross the great divide
To go from the land of the living
To the other side

I have not done all I can
To make the world a better place
To show the love of God
To demonstrate His eternal grace

But when the time does come
And I must from this life depart
My hope is in His Holy Love
Which I hold within my heart

THE GREAT DIVIDE

To all living
There is a great divide
That when we have crossed over
We must stay on the other side

On this earth we live
We lean to live and grow
It is what we have learned
That we generally know

When we cross that great divide
Out of this world of toil and sin
With those on earth
We can never interact again

FAITH

We come to a fork in the road of life
We can go either left or right
We make a choice based on hope
Walk along with all our might

It is by faith that the Christian walks
Along the path of life
Through the world of love and hate
Through this place of strife

Faith is the golden assurance
Faith and hope and love
That when we cross the great divide
We will have a home above

THE CHRISTIAN LIFE

In this world of toil and sin
The Christian doth shine
As a beacon to God
The devil to bind

The power that God doth have
Is grater than we can know
It is the power of love
That in our lives doth grow

The Christian life is a life to God
To follow in His way
So that we may forever live
As we do what ever He doth say

The Christian life is more than that
For we can become children of God
So that we may forever live with Him
When ere our body is beneath the sod

IN THIS WORLD OF TOIL AND SIN
(a song)

In this world of toil and sin
Where evil men do their will
My Savior came to us from God
God's Holy Way us to tell

From heaven God sent him
He came down us to save
Thought evil men him did kill
God raised him from the grave

God's wisdom is beyond all men
Into the world of sin
He sent his only Son
From Satan's power to win

(Course)
He sent his Son
He sent his Son
He sent his Son
The world he has won

AGAPE

What shall we liken the love of God to
It is more than we can ever know
So rare and holy in every way
It saves us from every woe

Would that we could love
As the way of God
But only One has ever been
To save us from the sod

The only way that we may know
That which is in the mind of the Holy One
Is to love in word and deed
To follow His Holy Son

For we may live a thousand years
A thousand years and a day
But never will we be able
Our soul's debt to pay

For thought we live in a world of sin
Immersed in our whole being is
By the death of the Holy Son
God will let us be forever His

Our sins may be washed away
By agape love
That can only be ours
By the will from above

There is nothing we can do
To deserve the love of the Most High
But by His love and by His Son
To His throne we may draw nigh

HEY, WHERE ARE YOU

Hey, where are you
Hiding from the hand of God
Hiding from what you've done
You can't hide, even beneath the sod

There is no hiding place
When God asks you where you are
For there is many a place
God's word is your guiding star

GOD SENT

God
God sent
God sent his
God sent his only
God sent his only Son

To save
To save me
To save me from
To save me from my sins

That
That I
That I might
That I might have
That I might have eternal life

I
I must
I must believe
I must believe in Him

TRUTH

When we see the world
The bad and the good
We know there are actions
Which we know that we should

There are actions of others
There are things which they tell
To make them feel better
But next to the actual, they pale

The truth is what we desire
From those with whom we deal ever day
If they do not tell the truth
We cannot believe what they say

Trust is built on truth
If ever truth is not so
Then we cannot believe
Or ever again know

THE END OF TRUTH

Where is the end of truth
When all will be known
When all that is finished
And all good sown

All is the providence of God
It is His Holy place
Those who find this rest
Will see His glorious face

So should live as though the end
Will come very soon
All that this world desired
Will pass into eternal ruin

DO OTHER PEOPLE TELL THE TRUTH

Do other people tell the truth
We can never, never know
But we can be sure of this
They will reap whatever they sow

To all comes the eternal truth
To the innocent and guilty too
As we to through life's long walk
We become what ere we do

So tell the truth in all you do
Deal false with no one
Justice will come in the end
When life's race you've run

TRUTH OF JESUS CHRIST

We live in this world of toil and sin
Not knowing the truth we could
That belongs to the gracious Lord
It is not what mind would

For the end of it all
The battles lost and won
Is in the hand of God
Who sent His only Son

We can but trust the message
Send by Christ to us
On how to live and how to die
And how to eternally trust

BEAUTIFUL WORLD

The beauty of the world
Is more than I can see
It would seem that God
Set the beauty just for me

I will not hurt others
I will be good to them
For they are also God's children
As much as I am

So we should live in peace
Peace for all time
For the will of God
Is yours and mine

STANDARDS

We live in a world filled with sin
A world which doth temptation bring
There are those who hate us
When of the Lord we sing

The world has standards
Standards some of which are wrong
They say "It's all right"
And sell us for a song

But God has given us standards
Standards of love and care
If we follow these standards
When we reach the end, our soul will be there

WE NEED A STANDARD

We work and we strive
We do right and wrong
Sometimes we sell ourselves
For little more than a song

We sell what we have
For a moment of pleasure
Then we live to regret
In the time of our leisure

To keep on a steady course
That will help you succeed
You need a goal, a standard
Bad actions to impede

So set your standards high
Also your goal
So your life will have meaning
Yourself will not be sold

NO ONE MAY NOT ADVISE GOD

No one may not advise God
On what He should do
For whatever God would have
Must be eternally true

Our eyes are temporal
Cannot see beyond our fate
But the eyes of God
Look at the eternal gate

We can but worship God
Can only serve and keep
The commands that He has given
Serve with will so meek

REMEMBER OUR CREATOR

Remember our creator
The great things He has done
So loved He our world
He sent us His only Son

To love and redeem
The human race
That now and forever
We may be called His kin

So love the Lord
And love our fellow man
That when to heaven we go
We can hear His great Amen

GIVE TO GOD THE HOLY PRAISE

Give to God the Holy praise
For the accent of days
For we have blessings
Blessings and praise

God sent His Son
To save us from sin
That when we have passed
It will be the victory we win

Our salvation He gave
Through death on a cross
That victory came
From what seemed a loss

Praise is all we can give
To Him who is on high
That by His holy will
To Him we may draw neigh

THE INSPIRATION FROM GOD

There are acts of faith
God would have us do
There are other good things
We would do if only we knew

Often times God does not appear to us
In a holy form
But God has told us what we must do
What He considers the norm

The word of God inspires us
To act according to His will
By following His precepts
We will not do eternal ill

So we may be inspired to act
By the will of the Lord
It shall always end in peace
Never in the deadly sword

Would that God did directly speak
To each when ever we should act
But the inspiration from God doth come
From His book, that's a fact

So act as the will of God
Does direct us every day
So that when we stand before His seat
We will know what to say

ETERNITY

Today is the first day
Of the life we will live
We march forward in time
To take and to give

But tomorrow, tomorrow, tomorrow
Tomorrow will never come
For when tomorrow comes
Another day will have run

But after the last tomorrow
There is a forever more
Where we spend this is God's decision
The result of life's chore

So parries God
Praise Him in every way
For eternity's tomorrow
Is for Him to say

THE FACE OF GOD

There are things which no one may know
Things that we cannot see
By the will of God
This is the way it has to be

Would that I could know all things
From the greatest to the small
But if I knew all things
My responsibility would be for all

God has given us His will
His revelation in the Bible we trace
But no one may see God
No one see His face

LOVE

When we were very small
On our mothers we did depend
It was to her loving arms we could run
Whenever the world on us did descend

As we grew older
The more of us we did become
We found that human love
Was more of life the sum

But the love of God
Is deeper than the sea
It is a caring of great expanse
That is for you, for me

FAITH

As we walk our walk through life
We must on others rely
For a person, by themselves
Will quickly wither and die

We know what we know
That is a solid rock
If it proves to be not so
It is a major shock

We can but live our life
With a solid base of faith so
That when we will see the truth
It will be what we know

So faith is the substance of what we can not see
The basis on which we believe a report
That when we hear the facts
Through them we can sort

Faith is the basis for life
The foundation's solid rock
There are those who say it isn't so
If true, then they will mock

But faith is our eternal guide
That the path we must trod
Will, at the end of life
Lead to the throne of God

WE ARE GOD'S

God can use every one
What ever they know
To do His good will
To make His will so

You cannot disrupt the will of God
It moves like a mighty hand
Along the corders of history
Throughout the wide land

So what must we do
To serve the will of God
We must strive to act this way
To bend to His holy rod

GOD

All around us, in every way
There is a silent reminder
Of the power which is creation
Of the one who is the sender

To know that God exists
That He has us in His care
Is to have His holy writ
To live in the world, here

For God is eternal
He set the world going
But for the mind of man
The power is in the knowing

JESUS

The world was waiting
For what, it did not know
So God in His love did send
His Son to help us grow

To be born of a woman
Is common to all
But if we depend upon ourselves
We are game to the fall

God's Son showed us how
To be of the spirit born
So that from the perverse world
Our spirits may be forever torn

At the end of our life
To heaven we may go
So at our God's feet
We may forever grow

But this life before the grave
Is where we now must live
To show those about us the way
That God's Son did give

So live as God would have you live
So worship Him as our Lord
For He has loved our world
And given us His Holy Word

FAITH IN THE FUTURE

The future we cannot see
It is a blank slate
But it will get here
All we have to is wait

There are things we wish
Things that are not now
It is this faith in the future
That we will know how

The faith in the future
Is the hope that we have
But what it will really be
Is what chance will give

If we do not have a goal
A place for which we hope
When the future gets here
We will not be able to cope

It is by the faith we live
That what tomorrow brings
Will be what we want
Our future, our things

HOPE

We live in a world
A world where things go bad
If this is all there is
Our future looks sad

We should not let it get us down
For today is not forever
Things will improve
Although it may seem never

It is this brighter future
Not the present dope
And God's eternal grace
On which we place our hope

GOD'S COMMISSION

I have been commissioned by God
To change the way we think
About the here and now
About our eternal link

If I follow His will
Do what He would have me do
I will be in His holy truth
Do what is just and true

So I will follow the will of God
From sun to setting sun
And do what I must do
When ere my race is run

CHARITY

Love your neighbor as yourself
Give to those in need
Follow the will of our God
Don't be overcome with greed

Love of all people is God's will
He who sent His only Son
So that by his example
To Him all may be won

For as followers of the Son
We represent what he taught
The terrible price he paid
Our salvation he bought

It is the love of others
Of the brotherhood
That is the charity we have
To give ourselves for the good

HUMBLE

Of what would you tell others
Of what are you proud
Make sure they all know
Tell it out loud

Is it something you've done
Or something you have
We all have such things
For which we're glad

But no one likes a proud spirit
One who will boast to all
They want someone who will listen
When on them they call

To be humble is to listen
To instructions from those who know
So that we may have a better life
As through life we go

God likes a humble spirit
One who knows their place
To those who will obey
God will bestow His Holy Grace

WE CANNOT KNOW THE WORD OF GOD

We cannot know the word of God
Unless we listen in prayer
For with every truth we hear
We must place our soul's ear there

The prayer of a repent man
Will listen as well as say
For God doth hear our needs
More than what we have to say

So pray to God our Father
The Father who is on high
That when we need Him most
His angels will draw neigh

THE WORD OF GOD

The word of God
Is the food for the soul
His Holy Bible
Will make our spirit whole

We can attempt
To bend it to our will
But then we are judged by it
It stands the test still

To know the Word of God
We must study and pray
For within it's Holy Word
Our life must always stay

LOSING OUR WAY

As we go through life
We make choices every day
If we make the wrong choice
We will lose our way

For there are many paths
That our life can take
We cannot make a different path
It is the choice that we make

Set your life's anchor
Set it on God's rock
Despite what the world may say
Ignore them when they mock

For God is our guide
He loves us in every way
In the final analysis
He will greet us on our final day

THE PASTOR

It is Sunday morning
We meet to hear some Holy Word
For during the week at work
It is not the word I have heard

I did not know God had a sir name
Nor that so many people called my Lord
That they wished to condemn so many things
Call down Hell by their word

Now we are in our church
Here to worship our God
There is no room for such talk
To give our soul the nod

So listen to God's Holy Word
That we may cure our soul
When we leave this place
Our spirit will be made whole

JESUS NAME

When ere we pray to God
We ask for what we will
But God, in His good grace
Gives us what makes our souls still

Jesus said to ask in His name
And he will give what ere we ask
But we need to be very sure
When we ask, we are in His will

For to ask in Jesus's name
Is to ask in the power of who He is
To know we must believe and do
To have our souls aligned with His

So ask in Jesus's name
But be very sure
That the glory given
Is to God

BUT GOD

As we contemplate our end
Buried beneath the sod
There are the words

BUT GOD

The good news to us
To each and every one
Is that God has for us a home
When our race on earth is run

Go forth with the message
Of power and of love
That when we ether live or die
It will be to the God above

The words are holy
Contained in the Holy Book
Apply to our lives
No matter where we look

So worship the God of heaven
The God of both you and me
That when we're at the end
The face of God we may see

HOW DOES THE MAN OF GOD

How does the man of God
Improve his daily life
To worship to the end
In life's ongoing strife

The way plain may be
For every one to go
But it is the holy person
Who the way does truly know

For we lift up our hands
To our Holy God
For when life's end does come
We'll all meet beneath the sod

But while we're here on earth
In this world of toil
Do not from any good dead
Your very being recoil

PRAISE BE TO GOD

Praise be to God
Praise Him in all the earth
He knew me in the womb
He was present at my birth

We can but praise the Lord
For His great love
Who sent His only Son
From heaven above

There is non other
That so loves us every day
So that when we most need Him
He is with us in the fray

SAVED FROM THE FALL

Jesus was born in a distance land
Jesus was born to be the Son of Man
Born to teach us how to live
Born to save us from the fall

Not by love, not by things
Are we saved from the fall
But by the will of God
Are we saved when He doth call

THE SUBJECT

The subject is God
The subject of our live
We may have many worries
But God gives men a good wife

There are many things
The world doth pull my soul
But by keeping my eyes on God
My future will be made whole

So I should discipline myself
In action, word and thought
I will find that in the end
It will be heaven that this bought

THE THREE

There are mysteries that we cannot know
We wonder how it can be
That our Holy God
Is one, yet three

God, the Father of all
His love is greater than we can know
By His will and by His might
He made the world so

God, the Son on earth
Who came to save us all
That we can from our faults
Be saved from the eternal fall

God, the Spirit within
The power of God in His church
That we may not know defeat
When we care for His people much

Three in one
One in three
We do not understand
But it is salvation for you, for me

WHAT IS A MAN

What is a man
What can a woman be
Is it how they look
Or what others see

We look at the outside
The clothing and what they do
But we cannot know their soul
Or know the world they knew

We are who we are
Inside as in our soul
We present a face to the world
We do actions so bold

But we will be eternally judged
By the Holy Supreme One
On who we are and what we do
Once our race on earth has run

ABOUT THE AUTHOR

Richard Gold was born in Bartow, Florida and attended college and worked for the Government for 40 years. He has been a Christian and writing poems for as long. Gold is now retired which gives him the time necessary to continue to write. Gold lives in Indian Head, Maryland with Penny, his artistically talented wife.